THE MONEY IS IN YOUR MESSAGE

I0465321

7 Steps for Authors, Speakers & Business Owners to Create & Monetize their Message Even While Sleeping

Barry Schimmel

John McCabe

www.Themoneyisinyourmessage.com

SPECIAL OFFER

The Money is in Your Message:

- Free One-On-One Consultation
  Spend 20-30 minutes working together to
  create a plan for getting your message out
- Everyone who applies for a consultation
  receives a gift

4 WAYS TO REGISTER

Mobile Text
Text to: 58885 your name and email with the
keyword **Bonusmoney**

Voice
Call 866-603-3995 PIN # 149315

Web
www.bonus.Themoneyisinyourmessage.com

QR Code

Table of Contents

Dedication

Barry ~

This book is dedicated to…

My parents, Burt Schimmel and Sue Hardman, whose guidance throughout my life was everything that was needed. They taught me to work hard, be honest, and follow my dreams.

My wife of almost twenty years, Jennifer, has always been an inspiration to me and to our two children. She has not only helped me write 7 books but always supported my efforts, making each journey purposeful.

My son Alec who is started a new chapter in his life as a college student. He is majoring in computer science with a minor in Spanish. He has made me so proud as a father and a friend. I love him dearly.

My daughter Elissa is a true leader in every sense of the word. She will be graduating high school this year as a Junior. I am grateful for every moment we spend together and looking forward to her next chapter. My love for her couldn't be greater. Proud daddy!

Thank you to all my clients for believing in me and making this possible. They stood by me during all my learning moments and I wish each of them the happiness and success they desire.

Barry J Schimmel

John ~

Having the privilege to share my story, to speak to the truths that have enabled me to do what I have always dreamed of doing, is due to so many that I encountered along my journey. I would need to write thousands of books to have the space to thank everyone who is responsible for where I am today. I must of course begin somewhere, so I thank each person that crossed my path. I am so very grateful to for everyone seeing and believing in me and my message.

Most of all, I thank my parents Gary and Shirley McCabe. They were supportive and encouraged me to be the person I am today, and not conform to society's norms.

They have provided me a level of joy and happiness that until now, I never knew was even possible.

John McCabe

Barry's Story

I grew up with a loving family in a tough intercity neighborhood of Chicago. Funds were tight and violence could easily be found. It taught me to be mentally and physically strong. It also taught me a solid work ethic. I knew that if I wanted something, I needed to work for it and I did. Cutting lawns, delivering newspapers, you name it, I did it. By the time I was in high school, I was helping my parents pay the mortgage. It really was about survival.

As soon as I graduated high school, I joined the Air Force and was eventually stationed in Germany as an SP. I had the honor to protecting the American hostages when they were released from Iran back in 1981. The Air Force taught me so much and I am proud to have served my country. The Air Force also gave me a path to get my college education. Once I was discharged, I worked full-time and was a full-time student. After receiving my Bachelor's degree in Marketing, I continued and received my MBA in Marketing at Roosevelt University.

Education, hard work, and a commitment to helping myself and others has been the theme of my entire life. For the last 25 years, I have successfully incorporated my strengths into the marketing and technology industries, building 3 multi-million dollar companies. Now, I work with others who have a mission and passion to continue to advance themselves, to contribute to others, and to leave a positive impact on the world.

John's Story

John A. McCabe is a 3 Time International #1 best-selling author, speaker, entrepreneur, business coach, consultant and real estate investor, John A. McCabe, has been helping entrepreneurs and businesses since 2004.

John has an impressive career as both a business consultant and real estate investor. Through his implementation of process, procedures, systems, technology, and personnel, he helped grow a company from $1.5 million to $7 million in just four years while dramatically increasing its bottom line.

John then started ioffersolutions Real Estate Services and within two years had been involved in controlling over $10 million worth of real estate, generating him a six-figure-per-year income without ever using his own money or credit. As a proud entrepreneur, John built his business by generating an abundance of leads and opportunities. By positioning himself and his business as the go-to company. Taking what has made him so successful in his business ventures, John has developed a formula that, when implemented, consistently yields results.

Originally from Windsor, Nova Scotia, the Birthplace of Hockey, he studied business at Acadia University then moved to Edmonton, Alberta, where he currently lives and works.

About This Book

Occasionally, a revolutionary idea, system, model or formula comes along that completely transforms the landscape of an industry.

This book is not your traditional marketing book, but rather addresses the number one problem every single coach, consultant, author, speaker, entrepreneur and business owner has right now… having a clear concise and consistent message that you can monetize with multiple streams of income!

My guess is you're here right now because you have a mission, a purpose, and a desire for a lifestyle change. You want control over what you do and how you do it. You're here because you want to dramatically grow your business, your brand, your income, exposure, serve more people or make a bigger impact in people's lives.

I know what that feels like. My passion has always been to help people grow their business by attracting more attention, generate leads and opportunities to get you out there following up, closing deals and making more money. If this sounds like you, then you're in the right place at the right time!

What if there was a simple and easy way to get ATTENTION with your message and get your prospects into one of your many streams of income?

What if you could make it happen IMMEDIATELY without getting bogged down with technology?

This book will introduce you to a system that creates an impact on your ideal target market, position you as the expert or authority in your business and accelerate your ability to make money.

By the time you finish reading this book and reviewing the FREE resources, you'll understand the underlying strategy behind the "The Money is in Your Message". You will have a blueprint that will assist you in implementing the strategy into your business.

As you read this book, we encourage you to open your mind to new ideas, strategies, and tactics. Push past limiting beliefs, be courageous in trying new methods, and remember that we are here to serve.

Part 1: Marketing Insights

The following section will provide an overview of key insights Barry has gained with his years in marketing and technology. Why is marketing mentioned here? Because you are marketing yourself to event planners, business leaders, audiences, etc. A general foundational base of knowledge is beneficial to positioning yourself as a expert people want to hire.

Some background on Barry:

Before opening my marketing company—Microshare Intl—in 2010, I had grown three multi-million dollar businesses. Prior to that, I received traditional training while earning my MBA from Roosevelt University in Chicago, IL.

While running my companies, I always knew that it was crucial to keep my finger on the pulse of my marketing. After 25 years, I've learned what works and what doesn't.

In that journey, I had to have clarity and continually stay current with new trends and insights. I learned from the most effective and cutting-edge marketers, and I executed countless sales and marketing campaigns.

This section is a glimpse of a myriad of books read; dozens of trainings, seminars, masterminds and coaching programs; and thousands of mistakes.

www.BarrySchimmel.com

Chapter 1: **Mindset**

Your Foundation for Success

It is essential to change your mindset to change your life.

Myth:

Mindset takes a long time to change, and the longer you have had a belief the more time it takes to revise it. This outdated view goes back to the early days of psychology and neuroscience, when scientists told us erroneously that our brains are hardwired, static and fixed like some sort of machine made purely of physical parts.

What is Mindset?

A set of assumptions, methods, or notations held by one or more people or groups of people that is so established that it creates a powerful incentive within these people or groups to continue to adopt or accept prior behaviors, choices, or tools.

Barry's Perspective:

Let me clearly explain why mindset is so important. I hear all the time how entrepreneurs are struggling and digital marketing doesn't work. The biggest complaint I hear is, "I have been burned so many times I don't trust anyone."

I can't argue with them because that is their experience. I can help them change their mindset when they follow a proven, systematic approach which delivers results.

With this foundational understanding in place, you must evaluate where you are now and where you intend to be a year from now (or even 5 years from now).

How to change your mindset

1. Gather information about your best clients to understand what problems you solve for them, and who they are. Also, find out what they love and hate and why they love and why they hate.

2. Analyze how your competition is converting new leads. The foundation of getting leads is optimizing your message so prospects can understand what problem you solve and your solutions.

3. Examine your beliefs about what you are doing and how you are doing it. You must identify what's not working so you can stop doing it and focus on what others are doing that is working effectively.

4. Create your vision with a clear set of goals which will shape your mindset to get the results you desire.

5. Create a message that is clear, concise and consistent throughout all your platforms.

6. Protect your mindset against the naysayers and people who want to drag you down. You also must protect it against poor information and against overload. Keeping your confidence is essential. So please stay on the right path, look to improve yourself and to help others along the way.

The truth about mindset

In my marketing firm, Microshare Intl, I have seen many businesses grow substantially—in influence and revenue—and it always started with changing the mindset of the business owner/entrepreneur. On the flip-side, we have also seen numerous companies fail because they were unwilling to change or did not believe in the new ways to do things. "The difference between success and failure was always in mindset".

Successful entrepreneurs can change their mindset, and in turn, influence their marketing and sales activities; unsuccessful ones don't. This is true in every industry.

Change the World & Make Money?

In my experience, all businesses (even the solo entrepreneurs) function for two reasons:

1. To fulfill a mission (think Mission Statement)
2. To generate revenues

Most companies try to accomplish both, but in varying degrees. As a generalization, not-for-profit organizations lean towards trying to fulfill a Mission, where small and medium size companies (which include Authors, Speakers and Entrepreneurs) focus on revenues.

Here are some great questions that I love to ask my private clients, and sadly most of them don't have answer for them:

- What do you love about your business?
- What legacy do you want to leave?
- What have you done in the past toward that legacy?
- What is your company's Higher Purpose?

(For example, create One Thousand Millionaires, "We all have a powerful message to share… To help others overcome.")

Your mindset is essential to your success. If you believe "nothing will work for you," your actions will align to that and it is exactly what you will get. If you believe that life is always changing and that you need to be open to learning (both via success and failure for yourself and what you see with others), the opportunities are endless for you.

In addition, remember that what you do is always about other people. If you don't believe that, you need to re-frame the way you think about your purpose. You must come from a desire to help people. Now this doesn't mean you don't get paid. There is a fair exchange in value, but having the mindset to provide solutions to prospects' needs changes everything from the words you use to the conversations you have. This applies to the deals you close as well.

Embrace the power you have in you. Learn, grow, and then learn some more. Commit to your goals and take action on what leads to success. For so many people, it's not who you think you are that holds you back – it's who you think you're not.

Mindset Case Study

Dr. Kris, a Chiropractor and Functional Medicine Practitioner, was looking to expand her successful practice. As part of our strategy development, Barry worked with her 1:1 and worked through the six steps to help her align her mindset to her goals. During this time, Dr. Kris had some profound "aha" moments.

She realized:
- Who she loved to work with
- Who she didn't want to work with
- What she loved to do and where her passion was.

Speak to Sell

Together, we worked to solidify her unique value proposition and started communicating her unique story to the audience she was looking to attract. She embraced focusing and conveying what set her apart from all the other Chiropractors.

In the end, Dr. Kris decided to focus on the practice area she loves most and where she can contribute the most to her patients, which is functional medicine.

She is speaking around the country to educate her audience on the benefits of functional medicine. This is how she positions herself as an expert and offers her online products and services.

Tactically, we built a graphical framework to illustrate her services and define exactly what problems she solves and get patients faster. The foundation of the framework follows this illustration:

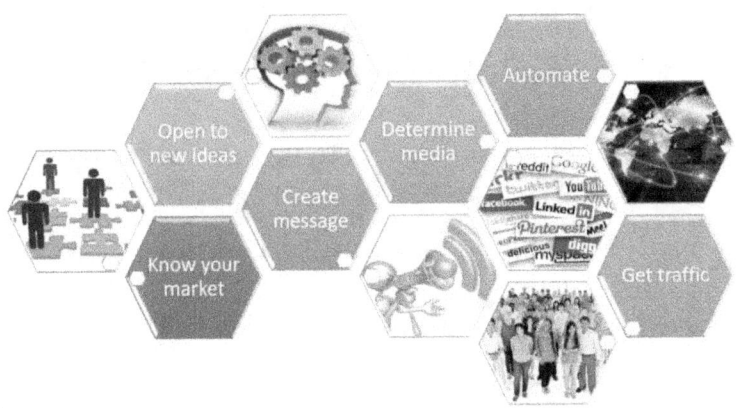

In addition, we helped her create a clear, concise message so we could target the speaking opportunities she desired.

This is where speaking came into the equation. understanding who she wanted to speak to and the unique problem she would help to solve.

Dr. Kris has a podcast show www.thegutsygal.com, regular online webinars, and a full schedule of speaking opportunities. Her new book is coming out soon.

Chapter 2: Evaluate Your Ideal Target Market

Target Market:

The market a company wants to sell its products and services to. This encompasses a targeted set of customers to whom it directs its marketing efforts towards. A target market can be differentiated from the market (as a whole) by geography, buying power/household income, demographics, and much more.

You are selling YOU – your products, your services, your expertise, your results, etc. As such, we will briefly go through some marketing principles that you should consciously integrate into what you do.

So, the question to you is where do you start:

- Market?
- Message?
- Media?

Where Do You Start?

Whenever I ask an entrepreneur or business team where they start their marketing strategy, 95% of the responses are incorrectly:

- 85% answer with Message
- 10% answer with Media

The most important element for any successful marketing campaign is understanding who you are selling to and what problem are you solving. Which leaves Market as the correct answer.

Part of understanding the market and how best to campaign involves gather information from your best client, as well as analyzing your competition.

Good communication skills are at the cornerstone of creating results since so much of your relationship with your client has to do with what you communicate, and not just what you do behind the scenes.

Listening is an art, after all, and not everyone knows how to do it properly. If you can master the art of listening, you'll improve your relationships by connecting with a deeper level of understanding.

Remember, your clients and audience care about the problem you are solving for them and will even share other problems they have that you might be able to solve. Keep the communication lines open, but focus on the right questions.

Market

Your upfront research in defining your target audience/market will save you time, money, and reduce your stress. Knowing your target audience is the first step to achieving the success you desire.

Factors to consider include:

- **Who are you selling to?**
  Demographics: Gender, education, profession, income, home ownership, geographic location, family, lifestyle, online activity, ideal qualities, and nightmare qualities?

- **What makes them want to buy?**
  Psychographics: Their wants, their innermost fears and frustrations, their objections to buying, and what would make them buy.

- **Do they have money?**
  Another big mistake I see with companies and entrepreneurs that are failing is spending their time and marketing dollars on a target audience that doesn't have the ability to pay for their product and services.

Evaluate Your "Ideal Target Market"

The success of your business can rely greatly on understanding who your marketing to and how you convey your message.

Knowing your ideal target market is the most fundamental aspect for creating and delivering a powerful message to give you the greatest odds for a successful marketing campaign. Remember, if you are looking to sell goods or services then it is important to know as much about your prospect as possible. We must get inside our prospects head and know what they are thinking, what problems they have and what solutions we offer to give them their desired outcome.

We forget sometimes that clients are giving us money in exchange for solving their problem. That's why getting inside their head is such a critical step for successful marketing. Most people forget they're communicating with humans and lose their sense of authenticity and genuine interest in them as people.

A lot of the time we tend to lump everyone together and use words like "them" or "they" when referring to clients. That's one sure fire way to lose the connection you have with your audience. We need to be more intimate in our conversations, in our messaging and in all our communication.

Whether you realize it or not, you naturally attract people with a combination of specific traits, beliefs and demographics. Generally, in most businesses you will find that 80% of the revenue and loyalty is found in 20% of your clients. That means that 80% of your energy is focused on clients who contribute to 20% of the revenue.

When you take time to identify the 20% of your clients who bring in 80% of your revenue and determine what they have in common, you can focus on attracting more of your ideal target audience. Having a clear, concise and consistent message will also repel those individuals who are not your ideal target market. You know, the ones who consume all your time for very little return. Imagine one single individual that represents your "ideal client" in all the messaging and write or speak directly to that one person.

This strategy is very powerful as it forces you to think specifically about your best client. It helps you use language that builds trust on a subconscious level and make them feel like the communication was written "just for them".

Targeting Your "Ideal Client"

When it comes to targeting your ideal client, you want to look at the 20% of the clients that provide you with 80% of the revenue and evaluate what common traits, beliefs, challenges and desires they have so you can zero in on those characteristics. When you know those commonalities, you can purposely create a message that connects with your audience on a much deeper level. This requires you to really understand who your prospects and clients are and are not.

Below is an Avatar worksheet for you to work through to get clear on your ideal target audience.

There are 7 key elements you will need to consider when creating a sketch and bringing your ideal client to life.

First, list all your target market's pains, fears, frustrations and ambitions that you've identified. You will want to make sure you have converted them into emotional and negative consequences from their perspective. This will help you when you you're ready to create your message.

Second, describe their ideal situation. Knowing what they would want if they could wave a magic wand and have the outcome they desire. Build a list of all the things that would be true if they got what they wanted. Outline everything in that picture if they could overcome the challenges they have right now. What would happen if they don't act now?

Third, gather some demographic information as well as their likes to narrow down the market. How old are they? What is their gender? Are they married or single? Pets? Kids? Occupation? Location? Income?

What kinds of things do they buy when they go shopping? What do they read and what kinds of shows do they watch? These things will help you visualize your ideal client when you are crafting your message.

Fourth, is the magic bullet they are seeking. What would the ideal solution be with respect to the problem they are facing right now? What do you feel they would immediately buy or invest in if it existed and you could offer it to them right now? Most people want to speed up the process of getting from where they are to where they want to be.

Fifth, is to create a list of 25 items from the previous 4 steps. From steps 1 and 2 you will want to identify 10 of the most important and relevant items. Then from step 3, identify 10 of the most important pieces of information with respect to your solution. From the fourth step, choose 5 of the ideas or concepts you wrote down from their magic bullet. From this you should now have 25 items that you can use in your messaging when connecting with your ideal target audience.

Sixth, is to give your ideal client or avatar a name. The more real you make them the more powerful it will be for you to create messages that connect with the prospects. Based on everything you know about them, what would be a good name for your avatar? Don't use a current clients name, try to come up with a new one and make the avatar unique.

The **seventh** and last step is to choose a picture of your ideal client sketch. The easiest thing to do is do a search in Google Images for the name you selected in step 6. Pick an image that you think would look like the ideal client based on their age and how you think they would look.

Going through the 7 key steps to bringing your Ideal Client to life will help you connect deeper when creating your message. Do not dismiss or skip over the work you need to put into identifying your ideal target market. It will be the most important foundation building process you ever do for your business.

Chapter 3: Structure Your Message

Money's in your Message...

As I mentioned in the previous chapter, one of the biggest hindrances to businesses selling more products and services is they don't really know their clients. Many of them never take the time to create an ideal customer avatar or determine what characteristics make up their very best customers. You know the ones who rave about you, your product, your services and even promote you to others. Those are the ones you want to attract more of into your business.

The businesses who say their customer is everyone are businesses that aren't going to be very successful. If you're trying to market your product or service to everyone, your message will get lost and resonate with no one.

How can you even begin to create messages, ads, or marketing material if you don't really know what makes your customer tick? This is one of the biggest mistakes businesses make when it comes to marketing. So many companies will just throw marketing messages out into the world hoping something sticks. Or worse yet, just blatantly ask for a sale without taking the time build a relationship and build trust.

The reality is that nobody cares what you have to say, whether it's at a party, networking event or speaking, unless it's relevant to them. Let's face it: there's so much noise in the world and so many people, brands and companies all vying for your attention. Messages come at you each day, don't register with your conscious mind. The same holds true for your potential clients. The only ones that really get through all the noise are the ones that make it through your "WIIFM" (what's in it for me) filter. In other words, the only ones you take notice of are brought to your conscious attention because there is some element that speaks directly to you or affects you in some way.

This means you've must communicate in a very powerful way that immediately gets the attention of your ideal target market. To do this, you first must realize the product or service you sell to your ideal target market is only a means to an end for what they really want. It's their desired outcome.

Your customers aren't buying the features of the product or service your offer. They are buying the result, their desired outcome and the benefits they receive from using your product or service. This means you want to focus on outcome, not what you do.

When you start to craft your messaging for your videos, interviews, live streaming, marketing, ads etc., focus on the results – the benefits they will receive using your product or service, the problems your business helps them solve. Eliminate any fears they may have you will help them overcome and the challenges they have faced up to this point.

A great exercise I learned from one of my past coaches is to ask yourself 3 simple questions with respect to your product or service. This aids you in positioning what you do from the perspective of the desired outcome or the benefits your ideal target market gets, instead of just describing your product or service. It also frames your offering in a way that is more compelling and relevant to your ideal target market.

1. What I/We do is…
2. What this means is…
3. What this really means is…

When you become clear on what it really means, and you start using the terminology in your day to day conversations when people ask what you do, or in your messaging when creating videos, going live or crafting copy for your social posts or marketing material, you will discover a shift in the attention you start to get from your audience or the people you are communicating with.

Creating Value Through Questions

In today's world, the human attention span is constantly decreasing. A Microsoft Study published in Time Magazine in 2000 showed the average attention span decreased from 12 seconds down to 8 seconds. Now, to put that into context, a goldfish has an attention span of 9 seconds. So that doesn't say much for us as humans.

When it comes to getting people's attention you have a very limited amount of time. In the marketing world you basically have 2 seconds to grab someone's attention. When you get their attention, they may give you 20 seconds of their time. When your message is on point they may give you 2 minutes. With compelling copy or verbiage, you can earn 20 minutes of their time, which is enough to influence and persuade them to have a relationship with you and do business with you.

As you can see, you only have the initial 2 seconds to cut through the massive amount of communication and messaging people get each day if you want to reach your ideal target market. Everyone has their "WIIFM" (what's in it for me) filter turned on and they ask themselves, "Who are you and why should I listen to you?"

For your messages to be effective and resonate with your ideal target market, you need them to really connect. One of the best methods to do that is to uncover and use their language, the language your ideal target market is currently using to have conversations in their mind. You also want to discover what decision triggers are making them buy. You can do this through surveys.

Surveying doesn't have to be complicated. It can be as simple as asking a series of questions that will provide you the feedback you're looking for. So, what is it you want to survey? What kinds of things are you interested in discovering and how can you use it to help you get their attention and move them to find out more from you?

The first things you should focus on when considering survey questions are around the pains, fears, frustrations and their ambitions with respect to the context of your market or the pain/problem they are trying to fix.

All individuals that are looking to buy something, or seeking a solution, are looking to move from their current state to their desired state. Many times, there are specific triggers that can cause an individual to seek out a solution. For example, if you are running cable from one room to the next and need a hole in the wall between the two rooms, most often you will require a drill. If you do not have a drill you will need to go out and buy a drill. However, it isn't the drill you really want. You aren't buying the drill to have a drill. What you really want is a hole, and to create holes you need to have drill. So, you aren't really buying the tool, but the result the tool provides.

All buyers suffer from pain, fear, and frustration, or have an ambition with respect to the problem you are trying to solve. It is your job to find out what it is and frame your solution as the answer to their problems.

Pain

Much of the time purchasing decisions are triggered by pain. An individual is having pain in a specific area of their life and they want the pain to go away. For a homeowner who has their home up for sale the pain may be that they can't carry the mortgage on their home any longer and it just isn't selling. They need a solution that will solve their pain immediately.

If you were someone who targeted homeowners who wanted to sell their home and were struggling with paying the mortgage, you would want to write copy that solved the pain they have and get them to their desired outcome, which is getting rid of the house and not have the financial burden weighing on their shoulders every month.

Another example, that successful Life Coach named Tori, who has 40 hours of client meetings booked each week and feels she is getting burned out. Most of the work with the clients is the same for each person at the same time of their training. Using her current model of one on one coaching, Tori's pain is that she has no time to fit any other clients into her schedule without sacrificing her personal time. Tori realizes she has maxed out her earnings using this model and is leaving money on the table because she has many other clients wanting to work with her.

In Tori's situation, her pain is that she wants to make more money, spend less time going through the same information with each of her clients and maybe even work less. As someone who coaches others on things like building digital products, delivering high ticket coaching, creating masterminds and workshops, I would address Tori's pains in a message that talked about how she can leverage her time, make more money working less hours and even make money while she sleeps. By understanding the exact pains Tori has, I can create messaging that will immediately gets her attention and get her to take action.

People don't care what you do, people only care about "What's In It For Them" (WIIFT). That means in your messaging you wouldn't say "I do this" or "I do that," but rather "You receive this" and "You receive that." It is such a subtle change but one that is very powerful to your reader or listener. Using the language, you receive from the surveys and speaking directly to one person in your messaging will increase your chances of getting someone's attention and get them to find out more.

Fear

Fear is one of the biggest motivators, we as humans have. We do whatever we can to avoid fear and have a fight or flight response when we feel threatened. So, when we are scared of something the majority of individuals generally avoid the situation all together. It's because of this that people aren't as successful as they could be, because they are scared to try or attempt things that would propel them forward.

Understanding these fears is great for marketing to your prospects. Knowing what people are afraid of with respect to their business or field of expertise and being able to communicate and offer a solution that helps them overcome those fears.

Let's assume you're a coach and help individuals with your specific field of expertise. You feel you have a lot to offer and give tremendous value to your clients who all love you and all see great success when they work with you. But you are currently charging very little for your services and struggle at the thought of raising your prices. You hear of many coaches, even in your field, charging between $5k-$10k per day for coaching with a client. But you are scared to even think of charging those amounts in that your clients will not want to work with you, they won't see the value, you will struggle to get clients.

For you, the coach, you are scared to raise your prices or to offer a high-end coaching program because you feel your market won't buy it, you don't know what to include or how to deliver something with such a price tag. For those reasons you are scared to move forward because of the fear of uncertainty.

As a consultant who teaches coaches on how to deliver high ticket coaching programs it would be very important for you to take into account all the fears their target market has when communicating their marketing message. In your messaging you would want to indicate you have a proven system for delivering high ticket coaching, a method for attracting and closing on clients in their coaching program and a way to over deliver each time. Provided your training program can in fact deliver upon these things, the messaging would resonate with the coach who wants to charge more but is afraid to do so. You just need to find out, through surveys, consultations and just talking with your ideal target market what their fears are with respect to your product or service.

Frustration

When people get frustrated they start searching out solutions or alternatives to what they are currently doing to alleviate their frustration. One prime example of that is if you are selling your high-ticket coaching program for $7,500 per day and you aren't making any money. Now your frustration may be that you aren't getting enough qualified leads or not closing any business, but bottom line you just aren't making the money you need to make.

Now, if you're frustrated because you aren't getting the qualified leads to convert into business, then you are probably looking for ways to improve that aspect of your business. Having someone who specializes in building a sales funnel that attracts high ticket clients and converts them into a consultation session is likely a good fit, and would solve the main frustration you have.

The key, for the person who builds and sells successful sales funnels that convert high ticket prospects into a consultation, is to know and understand the frustration their ideal target audience is facing. For example, you would want to know some of the language of the frustrated clients, know exactly what part is frustrating them and what they see as an ideal solution. Knowing these key pieces of information will enable the sales funnel consultant to be able to successful market to the frustrated high-ticket coaches out there looking to build and grow their business.

Ambition

The last and final reason people will be motivated or attracted to working with you and your solution is their desire or ambition. Their desire or ambition to reach their desired outcome is a very powerful motivator. It is what we are all striving towards as coaches, consultants, authors, speakers or entrepreneurs. We all have our goals, whether they be immediate, short term or long term, we are all trying to move forward and achieve them.

Your target market is generally looking to solve a problem. Some of those problems are in the form of ambitions, such as making more money solves the problem of not having enough money or having an online course solves the problem of not having enough time to train your clients.

Remember, it isn't the tool your ideal target market is buying, such as your course, your sales funnel, your coaching program; it is the result they ultimately want. People don't buy a drill because they just want a drill, they buy a drill because they need holes and the drill is the quickest and fastest way to achieve the hole.

Knowing the ambitions of your ideal target audience will enable you to attract more of them wanting to work with you, and ultimately buy your product, service or solution.

Almost all our private clients have discovered that their biggest frustration is they just aren't making enough money and their ambition is they want to make more money. One thing we've discovered in working with hundreds of businesses over the past few years is that their message is not congruent with who they are helping and how they help their target market. Until you gain clarity on the message, it doesn't matter how many people you talk to, your conversion rates will be relatively low.

When you gain clarity on your message and get it in front of other people will want to work with you. They see you as the person who can solve their problems, whether they be pains, fears, frustrations or ambitions. So, go out there and survey, talk to and list those pains, fears, frustrations and ambitions your ideal target audience has and then create messaging that will connect with them based on the information you received.

The answers you receive from the people you survey will become a powerful list of questions that you can use in your marketing. This list of questions will become a very key part of your packaging and promoting strategies as you move forward. The questions can be main topics for your videos, which will then get repurposed into articles, chapters in a book and much more. You're really going to be hitting the right market with this information as it's coming directly from your ideal target market. When you are incorporating these questions, and provide the answers in your messaging and marketing, you will almost come across as psychic because you are answering the questions your market is asking.

Asking these 6 questions will uncover your ideal target market's decision triggers and the language they are using, which you will use in your marketing, messaging and when creating your content to create a powerful connection. By asking questions you show your dedication to really serving your market. Many of the people who answer the questions will thank you for taking the time to find out what they really think.

Now that you've gone through the foundation components of what it takes to create impact, become the authority and create a message that really connects with your audience, it's time to put this information into action and move on to Section 2 where you execute the acceleration of your authority status.

Chapter 4: Seed Your Irresistible Offer

Remember, you can use this for webinars, emails, sales letters, speaking and you could even use it as the outline for your book!

Do it right and you won't have to sell...

When I started my business, I tried to sell everything to everyone. What I learned is that you must understand who your target audience is and how to offer value without giving away the store.

Once you are in the room with the right people, the ones who have a problem you can solve, you don't have to sell.

So, what do you need to do exactly? Start by understanding some the definitions.

Seeding is, "planting ideas and related terms in your prospects mind which gives them a vision of where they are now and with your products or services where they can be..."

A **unique selling proposition** (USP, also seen as unique selling point) is a factor that differentiates a product from its competitors, such as the lowest cost, the highest quality or the first-ever product of its kind. A USP could be thought of as "what you have that competitors don't."

Developing an Irresistible Offer has Five unique elements;

1. Communicate your unique selling proposition
2. Offer value so prospects can see the benefits
3. Has scarcity
4. Creates a sense of urgency
5. Prevents opportunities from slipping through the cracks

Communicate Your Unique Selling Proposition

Being honest about your efforts

There are countless ways in which to establish a sound and effective unique selling proposition, but whichever type you should implement, it should fit nicely within how your prospects see the world.

Here's what I mean by that; let's say your prospect is a "visually stimulated" person. You most likely will do best by using words like "imagine", "see how that would look".

I found that by describing my offer in a way that the prospect understands "saved me from myself", I was able to achieve far greater results and benefits from all my efforts.

As you already know, people have five senses to relate to the world that surrounds them: **smell, taste, touch, sight, and sound.** In general, every one of us uses a sense or two more than another to interact with our environment and to get information from it.

So, let's continue the process of developing a Irresistible Offer and remember... each element is designed to remind us of the importance of being honest with ourselves regarding being as thorough as possible from the beginning, all the way to the payoff of closing the sale!

Here is what we offered our clients.

Example 1

The Money is in Your Message!

Digital Training Course

Get in on the System that's PROVEN to add an additional $10,000 - $20,000 per month to your income!

- Learn how to create a **powerful and compelling message** that will attract high value clients.
- Discover how to **create value through questions so you attract your ideal client,** you know, the ones that need help!
- Understand how to **create a framework to position you as the expert and build your authority!**
- Learn how to **create up to 9 streams of income** so your revenue stream increases month after month.

We targeted Authors, Speakers, Coaches, Experts, Consultants, Small Business Owners, and Entrepreneurs and we focused on the pain point of making more money. We separated ourselves by having a proven 7 step proven process. **We packaged our product,** so it was unique as it adds different elements that are needed to give the prospect the highest probability for success.

Offer Value So Prospects Can See the Benefit

In example 1 we stated many benefits.

- Attract High Value Clients
- Value thru questions
- Position you as the expert
- Build your authority
- Create 9 streams of income

These are all the things you need to make more money and grow your business. This is the process of seeding. Stating what is needed to achieve the results they desire and letting prospects know that this is what you deliver with your products and services.

Has Scarcity

When you offer your product, you want prospects to understand that the price is for the fast action takers and offers a **Fast Action Bonus like below**

Fast Action Bonus Items

Receive a Proven Webinar Framework that helps you close sales **($399 Value),** and you'll also receive the Speaking Framework that will give you the structure you need in order to be able to put together a signature talk.

It is always good to limit the number of Fast Action Bonuses you are going to give away to create scarcity.

Creates A Sense of Urgency

The fast action bonus going away and the price going up creates a sense of urgency.

When you combine scarcity with urgency more prospects will decide quicker if the solution is right for them. It's important to note that once you create the urgency, stick to what you tell them. If you stated, the bonus goes away make sure it does otherwise you will lose the trust of the ones who purchased.

Prevents Opportunity from Slipping through the Cracks

The key to having an irresistible offer is to make sure that prospects who really want and need your product or services takes swift action. With the amount of offers and information being seen throughout the day you might be forgotten about. The best plan is to make your offer so irresistible that they decide on the spot.

Put your best offer on the table first and make it go away as fast as it came so your new clients realize they made the right choice.

Seeding

When we talk about seeding an offer we mean going through a process of educating your prospects about what is needed to solve their problem. We do this through a systematic approach.

The goal is to get paid for helping your perspective clients using your knowledge, wisdom and expertise. This method can be used on a one on one presentation, one to many, speaking on stage, webinars, seminars and workshops etc.

As mentioned earlier, it matters not which avenue of communication you are utilizing to get the decision maker to take swift action when you present your offer. You will be able to successfully draw them deeper into your message, by creating an authentic desire for them to want to know you better, and begin to convince them of your irresistible offer. As a reminder, know that you must never forget that you only have one opportunity to make a good first impression. Therefore, one must remain mindful at each step of the process to the importance of not forgetting what the objective is here – to get prospects to invest in your products and services.

Immediately after your salutation, the very first thing you should begin to establish is what you do and how it is that you do this thing differently than anyone else.

Next, follow up with a story of transformation.

Example story of transformation

When I first met Loren, he was speaking for the first time at an Engaging Speakers event. Loren did a lot of background research on the people who were attending the event. (Brilliant strategy).

When we met, and I introduced myself he started talking like he knew everything about me. He even knew where my mom was from. (Little freaky)

Soon after he became one of my private coaching clients and he had not committed to which direction he want to take. After many conversations he decided to focus on speaking.

Within one year he booked 135 speaking opportunities, was a best-selling author. "How to get Speaking Gigs Fast" and created an online program to go with it. Currently he is marketing events that he is putting together for speakers. He has a private coaching program, and a retreat package.

Loren is already making six figures, and driving a brand-new car. He found the love of his life and recently got married.

My point here is I did not talk about how I helped him and what steps he took to get there. This is where, so many people get it wrong. They talk about all the details when they are trying to impress prospects. What people care about is what's in it for them. They want to be transformed.

This is the process of seeding. Helping prospects see themselves transforming with your help!

Chapter 5: Authority

Reaching more people and IMPACTING others*!*

Reaching more people and IMPACTING others can be challenging. We need our message to reach others and for them to want to listen to what we have to say. Our message has to be scripted so we are speaking directly to resolving their problem. This is easy once we are recognized as someone who has credibility, expertise and authority.

Most of us don't feel we can be a recognized authority for a variety of reasons. What we fail to realize is that being an authority doesn't mean you have the most experience, have the most education, have the biggest business or client base. Not even how well we are known in our market. Being an Authority figure generally means we are recognized for having 2 very specific components:

1. A core competence in our business or field of expertise

2. Committed to serving others with our unique talents and gifts

Becoming the authority in our business or field of expertise is about positioning yourself as the go-to person in our industry. People will take notice of you, get to know you, like you and trust you. Let's face it, people do business with people they know, like and trust.

But how do you get there, especially if you are just starting out?

There are 2 things you should consider before starting on your journey to become the authority in your field of expertise.

First, what can you do that will give you "perceived" authority even if none exists?

Second, how can you craft your message, so it resonates with people and gets them to listen, take notice, share, engage and follow what you have to say?

In this chapter, I'm going to use myself in all the examples. I want to give as much transparency to the process and I can provide much more disclosure about myself versus my clients' experiences here. I also want to model for you, that as an entrepreneur, it's very important to be vulnerable and put yourself out there. I need to do what I proclaim if I want to impact change for the people I serve.

What you will notice is how I've been able to quickly position myself as an Authority in helping my clients get seen, get heard, get noticed and deliver a message that resonates with who they're trying to attract. This makes it much easier for people to want to do business with you, and changes the power dynamic so you won't be scrambling

Authority Quick Start

If you're just starting and don't have much experience, or many stories or accomplishments that illustrate who you are, who you help and how you help clients. You can leverage related experiences in other fields, jobs, volunteer work that can transfer and demonstrate the kind of person you are and the skillsets you have.

Another great way is for you to borrow authority from others by proximity. This is also called "Authority by Association". This means you find people who are considered experts or authority figures in your field of expertise and get your picture taken with them, interview them and even get testimonials from the people the market knows.

Authority by Association

Since 2011, I invested a great deal of money into courses, masterminds and coaches in the field of marketing. Because of successfully implementing many of the marketing strategies I've learned, I have had the opportunity to speak and be part of panels at the same events as these well-respected people in the marketing industry. Because of that I can make the following statement…

"I've shared the stage with marketing experts and influencers like Mike Koenigs, Ed Rush, Mike Filsane, Pam Hendrickson, Lisa Sasovich, John Assaraf just to name a few."

Now just from that statement, you can see I'm putting myself in the company of some very well-known people in Digital Marketing. So, even before I ever got started in my new field of expertise, I can create some authority for myself by proximity.

Think about any talks, discussions, events you were at where you were able to participate with some well-known people in your field of expertise.

Did you speak at the same event?

Were you ever on the same show or interviewed by the same person?

If not, try to find a situation where you can create this opportunity for yourself.

Now, let's look at some of the things I've accomplished in my past and how I can demonstrate why they provide value to others and how I can use them for my Authority Positioning.

John's Accomplishments

Prior to getting into Real Estate Investing in 2009, I worked for myself as an independent Business Management Consultant in the field of Business Operations.

From 2004-2009, I had 1 client in the field of Industrial Sandblasting and Painting industry based on Nisku, Alberta that I worked on 40-60 hours per week, except for a 6-month hiatus.

My accomplishment as an independent consultant is that I helped grow that company from 1.5M to 7M in just 4.5 years by implementing processes, procedures, streamlining operations, implementing technology, scheduling systems, project management philosophy, identifying individuals for key positions and much more within the organization.

This demonstrates my ability to:

- Take a high-level view of an organization

- Evaluate the operations

- Identify key areas that lack efficiency

- Create, implement and execute changes within the organization that have a positive impact on the company's revenues and expenses

Most companies require the same fundamentals when it comes to business; however, they all have minutiae differences and nuances. Most strategies can be implemented into various businesses regardless of their industry and still be effective.

When I went to consult the sandblasting and painting business. I knew absolutely nothing about the business of sandblasting and painting. I had come from the corporate world of payroll processing, software systems and project management. Fortunately, much of what I learned about systems, project management and technology was transferable to other businesses.

By taking the role of the observer, asking questions, watching people and the operations of the company as a whole for the first week, I was able to identify which areas had the largest room for improvement and the biggest impact on the bottom line. I then went ahead and implemented the strategies, systems and philosophies into the business that made an immediate impact in the business.

In the very first month of a business that was grossing $1.5M per year, most of it in a 6-month window, I was able to add $50,000 to their bottom line NET figure just from implementing strategies I learned in my other career. I increased their yearly Net Income by 3.33% in just one month! For a company that was going in the RED each winter, that was huge.

I created a domino effect within the company. The increase efficiency enabled them to make more money, push through more projects, give the workers steady work, decrease labor costs, increase productivity, make more money, build their own state of the art facility, and then increase everything all over again. Even expand into other markets.

This example, hopefully gets my point across: Many of the skills you have, and accomplishments you've achieved in your past, can play a big part in your **Authority Positioning**. When you're first getting started in your new business or field of expertise, this is an effective strategy.

Now, let me bring this back to the context of positioning myself as an Advisor, Coach, Consultant in the field of Accelerating Your Authority. My background accomplishments of implementing strategies, systems and blueprints to dramatically grow a company over a very short period of time added massive credibility to myself in a business field where I was just getting started.

Helping you **Accelerate Your Authority** in 100 days or less comes down to implementing a very specific system, strategy, blueprint or formula. I've already demonstrated in that one example I can create and implement systems that can have an immediate impact on a business in the short term, as well as grow it in the long term.

Therefore, my question for you is: What transferrable skills and accomplishments can you use in your business? For those who have been in your industry for some time and want to position yourself as the authority, then show or talk about examples of helping your ideal target market achieve their desired outcome.

The skills you have that are directly related to the field of expertise or industry you are going into is much easier to link with accomplishments.

My goal is to help you generate exposure and awareness in a very short period of time, so you can generate more sales, make more money and make a bigger impact in people's lives. You might be thinking...

"Ok John, where's your authority in being able to do this? Where is your authority in the field of creating and accelerating authority for someone or a business?"

For this example, we are going to take a look back at my real estate investing business. In the recession of 2009, I was given 1-day notice that my services with the sandblasting and painting business would no longer be required. I had been self-employed for about 7 years and times were tough. Consultants and even employees weren't getting hired in my field of expertise at that time. Fortunately, I had just taken 3 real estate investing training courses, so I decided to give that a try. However, I had one big issue... I am an introvert. There was no way I was going to cold call people or knock on doors to try to convince homeowners they needed my service. In addition, that modal would not yield the revenue potential I needed right out of the gate.

I had to figure out how I was going to get people to contact me, set meetings with me and want to do business with me. Sound familiar? Fortunately, I'd taken some internet marketing courses in the early 2000's when I started a different business that primarily used the internet. I knew what it took to rank for SEO, what platforms to use for building a decent looking website, how to write effective copy that would get people to act, and where to spend the majority of my time to be most effective.

The very first day as a full time Real Estate Investor, I was receiving emails and phone calls from my ideal target market. I was getting homeowners wanting to book appointments and have me come and discuss the options available for their home. I was getting more leads in one month than most of my investor friends in a whole year.

From there, I went on to write 2 international #1 best-selling books in real estate investing, created 2 brands that are well known in the Canadian Real Estate Investing space, and built and sold marketing systems for other real estate investors. In addition, I created the marketing system and material for a nationwide rent to own company and coach real estate investors on how to generate more leads and opportunities for their business.

This example demonstrates that with the right tools, you can get yourself positioned very quickly and have great momentum in driving your business forward.

The big takeaway from all these examples is that before I even start helping people with my Authority Acceleration Blueprint or formula, I already had authority for myself from past experiences and accomplishments. I'm confident you can do the same thing for yourself.

Chapter 6: **G**enerate Multiple Streams of Income!

Now that you have reached this point, you should have a good understanding of how to position yourself and get create opportunities with your irresistible offers. With that foundation in place, it's time to get a clear vision on why you need multiple streams of income!

This chapter covers many **streams of income** that you can offer to your prospects to help more people and make money while you sleep. The goal is to have the ability to continue to serve high value clients and being able to get more prospects into your sales funnel at different price points.

Monetization Stream 1

We talked about creating authority. What is one of the fastest way to position yourself as an expert in your field?

Writing a book and getting it published

To start with, you have brilliance inside of you that needs to get out. You have life experiences and a different perspective compared to other in your field of expertise. Potential clients can't wait for you to share.

There are many ways to create an income stream from your book and I will share a couple of ideas with you.

1. Sell it on Amazon
2. Sell it at events
3. Sell it at your workshop
4. Market your products in it
5. Market your services
6. Have an event planner buy 100's

These are only a few ideas, and it might get you thinking about how valuable writing a book might be.

Your book will be your shortcut to becoming an accredited expert practically overnight. Launching and publishing a book will get you instant opportunities. Think about how much additional income a book might bring you. Will you get more high value clients because of your positioning?

Do you want to become a best-selling author?

The benefits of becoming a best-selling author are plentiful. Once your book reaches the best seller status on Amazon they will market your book. Amazon is a powerful marketing machine which you leverage for all the additional exposure.

A well-coordinated and executed book marketing campaign will help you get massive exposure among your peers, clients and raving fans. A well-run campaign can potentially expose hundreds of thousands, if not millions, of people to your book and your brand.

Once you become that bestselling author, you'll be able to receive fees for your speaking engagements. You also can appear on stage along with other high-profile speakers and that just raises your own profile even more. Now that you've reached that "EXPERT STATUS", it's much easier for you to increase your fees on your consultancy services and coaching packages. In fact, if you don't charge high enough prices for your services you could lose credibility.

The fact that a lot of people bought your book to raise it to bestseller status is proof that you have something to say worth listening to. This will make filling your LIVE events a breeze … in any economy.

If your book marketing campaign is well managed and successful, you'll find a series of top joint venture partners more than interested in promoting your book and services to their own clients. Running a successful book marketing campaign on Amazon, offers an INCREDIBLE opportunity for you to increase the number of subscribers to your list. The magic of Amazon is to get that hungry crowd back to your own website to start a long-lasting relationship with them and let them know about your other products and services.

If you're strategic in the way you craft your book marketing campaign, you can find yourself with a massive new group of potential clients begging to know more about you.

Monetization Stream 2

Speaking is an extremely valuable tool that can help you achieve great things in your business.

How many times a MONTH do you feel you can get booked to speak?

How much do you can get paid at each venue?

Would that be worth adding to your services?

If you answered yes, keep reading or go to the next monetization stream.

Speaking will not only help you make more money but there are many facets of your life that will benefit. Your career or your business is one of the places where public speaking is more beneficial than almost anywhere else. Using strong public speaking skills can give you a great leg up over your peers and over people you're competing against for different positions.

Public speaking can help you impress your prospects. You can make a great impression if you're confident in giving presentations in front of a crowd. Event planners might choose you to give more opportunities in future because they know that it's going to make them look good. You can be seen as a thought leader and a stand-out performer. Be confident and capable of getting up in front of a crowd and you could be seen as one of the best thought leaders in the area of your expertise.

Standing up and sharing your expertise will make people perceive you to be better than your competitors and they have an opportunity to get to know, like and trust you.

Being a keynote speaker will create context in your professional network and you will be more likely to have others promote you as the go to person. You're more likely to be seen by your target audience if you're able to speak in public and get up in front of a crowd. This creates context and a relationship – even if not a one-on-one relationship – so they can now interact with you.

They understand who you are. So, when a opportunity comes up and they're thinking about who can help them you will stand out because they know who you are. Public speaking also helps you expand your professional network. You can inspire greater change and be seen as an effective public speaker, and you will likely get more of those opportunities to get hired as a speaker. Public speaking is great at building your self-confidence. It's difficult at first because public speaking is so scary. You feel so awkward or you don't like the way you sound.

But you will build confidence in the way you present yourself over time. It allows you to be confident not just in a public speaking situation but in a variety of social situations. You can be prepared for things like business meetings and networking events. You can also learn to think and act on the spot. Being good at thinking on the spot and "winging it" when you go into social situations will make you feel less stressed because you'll know that you can handle whatever happens. Build your self-confidence and get positive feedback or constructive criticism from people. You can then continue to grow and become better at communicating.

I think you get my point that speaking will make you more money and add value to you and your business in many areas.

Monetization Stream 3

As a successful business owner, you've probably spent years building a reputation as an expert in your field. Whether you're a successful entrepreneur or a author, speaker or coach, you have much to share with your existing customers and prospects on how they can benefit from using your products and services.

An educational seminar or **workshop** is one of the most valuable tools you can use to share your expertise, build credibility and establish yourself as an expert in your field. At the same time, you're generating exposure for yourself, developing new relationships and ultimately growing your business.

How much revenue can you generate from a workshop?
How many workshops can you put on in a year?
How much revenue will that add to your income?

Creating and selling workshops is about much more than just teaching clients something. It's part of a larger business strategy. You have heard the saying that it's easier to keep an existing client than trying to go out and find a new one. Your goal here is to really add value to those attending your workshop so they can't wait to hear about what else you have to offer.

Think through your entire product or service offering and make sure they understand what problem you solve and what they can purchase from you next.

Your number one goal is make sure you are adding so much value and giving the attendees your best stuff to help them achieve something new as the result of being there. People learn best by doing, participating and actively constructing knowledge. The more skill building activities you create, the more likely they will walk away having learned something new.

Your workshop will be an amazing marketing tool as it will increase your creditability and their trust in you and your business.

It's important to price your workshop correctly as people who attend for free are not normally your optimal target market. You want clients who have skin in the game and who are there to participate and get the most out of the event.

Monetization Stream 4

Digital products like a **Digital Course**, are increasingly attractive because of their low creation costs (your primary investment being your time and expertise) and inherently scalable nature.

Do you want to make money while you sleep?

If yes, would it be worth your time to create?

How much additional income do want to make each month?

To me, selling digital products is by far the most attractive online business. They're infinitely scalable once you create the products, you have almost zero associated costs for each unit you sell, and if you do a great job of promoting your products you'll be able to rank high in organic search results and bring in new customers at a very low cost.

You need to be considering how you can sell digital products with your business. If you have a valuable skill set, think of ways you can package your services as do-it-yourself online courses. If you're an experienced coach, perhaps your more junior counterparts would be willing to purchase templates from you. If you're an expert in any field, I can guarantee there are people who will pay for an accelerated learning experience through digital guides and instructional videos.

Monetization Stream 5

If you are looking to make your industry better and want to create a movement a **Certification Course** will be the way to go.

A certification course will position you as the go to company and against the competition you will stand out from the crowd. When prospects are doing their research and the competition is stiff and you offer a certification course which trains your competition you are at a definite advantage.

Your business advantage is that it plugs you into two new communities: one that is earning the certification, and one that has the certification. For example, if you are going for your PMP certification, you will immediately have something in common with other hopefuls, and this can provide networking opportunities through classes, the web, and meetings. The same holds true when you have earn the certification; you are a member of the "club." While these are benefits of PMP certification, the same would hold true of most certifications.

Gives you confidence that you have "passed through the chairs." When you have set your sights on a goal, put together a plan, work hard, and you reach it, you gain confidence, which spills over into all aspects of your life.

You can be a better mentor. The ability to mentor is based greatly on experience, but the best mentors can reach beyond their experience. They are able to extrapolate from their experience, and relate it to someone else's entirely different experience.

Gets your foot in the door in the new area. Many career changers turn to certifications to get themselves into a new area. For example, many marketers who want to advance will earn the certification to move into a position of authority and to help take their clients to the next level by learning a using a proven systematic approach.

This is more of an advanced approach to help bring higher quality services to your industry.

Monetization Stream 6

If you want to create revenue streams that grow month over month, one of the ways to accomplish the feat is with a membership site. You can charge a monthly fee for the valuable content you create. Remember, knowledge is power and your wisdom that you share is priceless.

When you are offering a product, or content through a membership site, your customers are paying you for the right to access your content for a fee.

Quite often the most successful membership sites start off by offering tremendous value in the form of free content. This helps in building a large FREE membership base and quickly earns the trust of the members who have already been acquainted with the quality and value of the products which are being offered.

Thus building this base of loyal members makes it much easier to offer "premium" paid content in the future which also secures a steady stream of income.

We mentioned earlier how a membership site can lay the foundations for a loyal customer base which is quite often based on trust.

After all, when people sign up to become members of your site whether it be a free or paid membership, they are entrusting you with their email address and their time and money.

For instance, when people sign up as members of your site they are usually doing so because they are specifically interested in what you have to offer. Therefore your membership base is the most targeted and fertile ground for your campaigns. As long as you don't overdo it, you can more easily convert very well when offering future products and services to your members due to the targeted nature of the audience.

By offering your content via a membership site, you in a sense ensure that only those who are interested in it will have access to it – simply because they went to the effort of signing up and/or paying for it.

In the world of the internet nothing is 100% safe from being stolen or copied but spammers or other shady visitors who want to steal or copy your material will be less likely get access to it because they usually will not want to sign up and pay for it.

As we mentioned earlier, you can make money while you sleep.

Do you want to add residual income to your company's revenue?

How much do you think your clients will pay?

How many clients will you get?

How much revenue will a membership site add to you?

Monetization Stream 7

People are spending more money on Coaching One on One than Internet Marketing and Direct Mail combined. Even when the economy was in a slump coaching was predicted to grow by 83% by 2018.

Does adding coaching to your business make sense?

One of the biggest advantages of coach is that it is very high in terms of net profits. I've certainly experienced that in my own business. The reason why it is so profitable is that your overhead is low. You don't need a lot of equipment or very much office space. I work out of my home office which saves even more money.

The only equipment that is needed is a laptop, paper, pen and a telephone. The fact of the matter is that if you sell any "How To" information right now, you really need to add coaching to your income stream. The goal here to make to setup a systematic process that is repeatable and gives you the ability to repurpose your content. I explain more about that later.

Coaching is going to be one of the most profitable areas of your business and I'll give you some reasons why.

Your clients will be paying monthly and will stay with you for a long time and you won't always be looking for new clients. Your revenue will be more consistent, which will reduce your stress. You don't want to be on a rollercoaster ride with your cash flow.

Another reason to add coaching to your services is that you can set your own hours, so you can spend more time with your family. That's enough of a reason for me.

Coaching you can start implementing today and have a solid stream of income coming in within 90 days. How does that sound to you?

When you add this model, so you don't have to worry about technology, which will probably reduce most of your stress right there. I use skype, and that's the extent of my tech if they are not local or meeting in person doesn't work out. This approach is not that complicated.

If you model your coaching program properly, you will have a stress free. Low tech. fun life and happy and satisfied clients as well.

Monetization Stream 8

Our next stream of income is Coaching, One to Many. Some of your prospects might not be ready or can pay for individual coaching. This is an alternative that will be good for both you and your clients and prospects.

Our goal is to not only add another stream of income but to help your clients get results, which will funnel them into your other streams of income. It gives them what they want and need at the same time it helps you build a relationship with them.

The preferred way of delivering this coaching is online using a program like Skype or Zoom. The technology is simple to use and very affordable.

Now let me ask you one question. Do you know anyone you can call today to get in your One to Many Coaching Program?

At the end of this chapter I will tell you how to get the bonus video.

Monetization Stream 9

Retreats are one of the best ways for business owners, executives, clients get out of their everyday run of the mill environment. A Retreat is an intentional time away to learn while being in a relaxing environment where you'll meet like minded people.

Honestly, this is where I gather my best ideas and start creating additional streams of income.

Our day starts out with a light breakfast while everyone gets acquainted. Then we are going into the workshop specifics in the morning and in the afternoon, we go on a excursion and do something adventurous. Something everyone would find enjoyable and relaxing. One we get back and clean up everyone can decide to go on their own for the night or get together for dinner.

The goal is to spend three days accomplishing what we set out do. My clients have their funnels designed and setup or an outline for their book with a pre-launch of their book to make them a bestselling author.

One of my favorite retreats is helping design an Online Program which they start creating and selling right away.

There is nothing better than taking a little vacation somewhere beautiful while learning, creating streams of income and accomplishing something that will help you and your business grow.

Don't forget to get your bonus at **www.bonus.Themoneyisinyourmessage.com** as I put together a video on the 9 Streams of Income that will give you a clear picture on the additional income you can add to your business to live the life you deserve.

Chapter 7: Evaluate

Let the future tell the truth, and evaluate each one according to his work and accomplishments. The present is theirs; the future, for which I have really worked, is mine.

- *Nikola Tesla*

I really believe that the core fundamental key to your success is to **Evaluate** your progress until you have a predictable and consistent revenue stream.

We get so busy working in our business that, we forget to work on the business. Do you have the discipline to evaluate and know your numbers?

Do you understand which services you offer help your clients the most and which skills you have that will transfer into profit?

It's not always how much money you make, but how much you keep. Evaluate, what it cost you to get a new client what the lifetime value of your client is.

One struggle that I see quite often with businesses is that they do not have enough up-sells and down-sells. Once you have a client that know, likes and trusts them, it is a lot easier to offer other services.

This is an area to keep an eye on and evaluate which services your clients and prospects want. My clients will tell me exactly what they want and how much they are willing to pay. Another way is to survey them and ask them directly what they like the best and what they want more of. What additional services would help them achieve their goals, dreams and desires.

Another way I evaluate what is happening in my business at any point in time is looking at my spreadsheet. It has my goals and projections for each month and year over year. I compare that with actual results within each of my different streams of income in order to understand where I need to focus or spend more time prospecting and closing business.

This also lets me predict slower times of the year where I can add more speaking engagements and workshops. Also, I can setup ads to get clients into my online programs and start making more offers.

Do you have a spreadsheet setup?

Do you have multiple Streams of Income?

Do you consistently **Evaluate** your business?

Do you have a Coach?

Do you attend a mastermind?

I hope I gave you lots of value and things to think about. Millionaires and Billionaires know their numbers and I know you will too!!!

Conclusion

We started our journey together by working on your mindset. When you open your mind, and get out of your own way, great things start happening in your life.

Our goal was to help you get your message out to the world and make sure you're not the best kept secret around. To accomplish this, you must understand your market, message and the media that's going to be used to make it effective.

Positioning yourself as an expert in your field makes it easier for you to stand out and be noticed. The clearer your message is and the more targeted audience you have will create demand for your services.

The key to success is having multiple streams of income so you can create predicable streams of income and make money while you sleep.

Making sure your follow-up process is flawless will help project your professionalism and you will close more business.

Knowing exactly where your revenue is coming from and your profitability is key to long term growth and stability.

Once you understand and implement what you have learned in this book, you are on your way to leave a legacy that will last forever!

Don't forget to get your bonus at **www.bonus.Themoneyisinyourmessage.com** as I put together a video on the 9 Streams of Income that will give you a clear picture on the additional income you can add to your business to live the life you deserve.

Other Books by Barry

All five of Barry's books reached the Amazon #1 Best Seller list, the Amazon International Best Seller List.

HOW TO GET SPEAKING GIGS FAST
The Ultimate Formula to Getting Paid

Digital to Dollars
How to Get Clients Fast
and Achieve
Unstoppable Growth!

*7 New
Marketing
Rules*

*Success
Junkie*:
12 Principles for
Winning the Life
of your Dreams

Barry Currently Speaks on…

"The Money is in Your Message"

- Learn how to create a powerful and compelling message that will attract high value clients.

- Discover how to create value through questions so you attract your ideal client, you know, the ones that need help!

- Understand how to create a framework to position you as the expert and build your authority!

- Learn how to create up to 9 streams of income so your revenue stream increases month after month.

"How to get Speaking Gigs Fast!"

- Lean how you reach event planners quickly and know what to say so you get yourself BOOKED!

- Discover how you can get paid telling your story, and how to price yourself for speaking gigs.

- Find out what it takes to stand out from the competition, so you increase your bookings.

- Know the best spots to look so you find speaking opportunities that are perfect for you.

"A Message to Entrepreneurs"

- It's no longer about economies of scale, but economies of speed

- It's no longer about getting money but giving value

- Today collaboration beats competition

- This wave has only just begun, and as with any wave, you can sink or swim

"Dream Bigger"

- Managing mindset

- Overcoming limiting beliefs

- Your circumstances aren't your destiny

- Protecting your confidence

"Thinking for a living"

- Creating new ideas

- Creating celebrity

- Living with purpose

Discover How to "Get Unstuck"

- Stuck is a myth

- Dial in your marketing

- Create the kind of freedom and income you've been waiting for all your life

- The superpowers that will get you through

In my life I've learned that true happiness comes from giving. Helping others along the way makes you evaluate who you are. I think that financial freedom is what we're all searching for. I haven't come across anyone who didn't become a better person through helping others become independent.

Congratulations!

It is time to first celebrate your victory. You created a goal of finishing this book, and now you have accomplished it. It is very important to take time, even if it can only be a moment, to celebrate your victories.

Recognize that you are one step closer to reaching your Vision. Know that we are proud of your success and very grateful that you took the time to learn and consider how you are going to implement our teachings.

Your next step is to nurture these lessons and then take massive action!

"Inaction breeds doubt and fear. Action breeds confidence and courage. If you want to conquer fear, do not sit home and think about it. Go out and get busy"

~ Dale Carnegie

To your success!!!!

www.ingramcontent.com/pod-product-compliance
Lightning Source LLC
Chambersburg PA
CBHW071523220526
45472CB00003B/1134